Transformative Innovation in Education

a *playbook* for pragmatic visionaries

Second Edition

Graham Leicester
Denis Stewart
Keir Bloomer
Jim Ewing

Contents

Preface — 5

Introduction — 8

Education for a Changing World — 11
  Shift Happens

The Dynamics of Long Term Change — 15
  How Shift Happens
  Three Faces of Innovation

The Limitations of 'Standards-based Reform' — 22
  Shifting Education

**Transforming Education:
Scotland Case Study** — 26
  Scotland's Opportunity
  Curriculum for Excellence
  Enabling the Strategic Conversation
  The Emerging Landscape of Education in Scotland
  Tensions in the Transition Zone
  Ostrich or Eagle? Dealing with Dilemmas
  Exploring the Dilemmas of the Second Horizon

Practical Approaches To Transformation — 41
  From Insight To Action
  Three Horizons Kit
  Getting Into Action
  Results

The Policy Framework — 52
  Making Space for Pragmatic Visionaries
  And finally

Preface

THIS is the second edition of a book first published in the spring of 2009. Since then it has sold well, going through a number of reprints. Its message has resonated with readers around the world: given the right kind of guidance and support, our institutions of education are perfectly capable of instigating the kinds of radical changes they need to make in order to prepare our young people for an uncertain future.

It is a message of practical hope, all the more attractive for being so rare.

Throughout the developed world school systems are facing the same challenge - to prepare students for 'jobs that don't yet exist, using technologies that have not been invented, in order to solve problems we don't even know are problems yet'.

Yet no school system in the world, so far as we know, has adequately addressed this challenge, even though all of them know they must do so. McKinsey's recent report on school improvement[1] reviewed three decades of international educational reform efforts and concluded: 'Lots of energy, little light'. Most OECD countries, it noted, 'tripled their spending on education in real terms between 1970 and 1994. Unfortunately, student outcomes in a large number of systems either stagnated or regressed.'

Clearly the challenge is going to take a special kind of innovation. We can't serve unknown future needs simply by squeezing the last drop of performance or efficiency out of the systems we already have - even though the political clamour, especially with budgets under strain in the wake of the financial crisis, is to do precisely that.

Incremental innovation is necessary but not sufficient. We also need 'transformative innovation' - innovations, starting at small scale, that have the capacity over time to transform the system itself to deliver outcomes the existing system cannot even imagine.

The first edition of this book contained a simple recipe for how to encourage such innovation: give professional

Transformative Innovation in Education

staff, school leaders, local governments, parents and pupils the tools, prompts and frameworks to encourage them to think beyond the constraints of the current culture and support them to move towards more radical aspirations. It introduced the first such support in the form of a Kit to enable schools to conduct the kind of far-ranging, future-facing, strategic conversation that must underpin any programme of lasting change.

Three years later we are able to update the text with news of substantial practical progress. In partnership with the Scottish inspectorate of schools, Education Scotland, IFF has developed significant new resources and a new stance specifically designed to support transformative innovation in a highly decentralised, bottom-up, system-wide approach.

The 'Opening Up Transformative Innovation' kit provides a simple way for any school to engage with an uncertain future - the challenges of a changing world, changing policy and changing young people.

The 'three horizons' framework on which it is based allows everyone free rein to share their concerns about the present system, to admit deeper aspirations that might be frustrated or under-realised today, and to design a 'second horizon' transition strategy to shift the system in that direction.

The whole conversation is grounded. This is not 'blue skies visioning' but hard-headed engagement with often uncomfortable facts about changes in the real world. But it also allows space for inspiration. Once a desired future has been imagined we can always find glimpses of it in the present. It often shows up in the shape of inspirational stories of practice elsewhere... perhaps even in the classroom next door. Everywhere the Kit has been used it has had the effect of unleashing pent up energy: 'we could try something like that here!'

And, working with Education Scotland, we have been able to capitalise on this opening up by introducing other

Preface

powerful frameworks for moving from insight to action developed by our IFF colleague Jim Ewing. These are described in a substantial new addition to the original text on 'practical approaches to transformation'. The approach has yielded impressive results across a range of schools of all kinds and all abilities – and is now being piloted in other jurisdictions outside Scotland, including Australia and the US.

It is clear that in today's complex and fast-changing world an approach to school improvement based on directive central planning can do no more than ensure acceptable minimum standards. By contrast, McKinsey suggest that the pinnacle of school reform, the final stage of the journey 'from great to excellent', will only be accomplished when the locus of improvement shifts from the centre to the schools themselves.

Our experience is turning the logic of that staged approach to excellence on its head. In Scotland we have given all schools the frameworks, the prompts and the support they need to bring the future meaningfully into their conversations about school improvement, and then to take the radical action such conversations suggest. This is a simple infrastructure for transformative innovation that, three years on from our first publication, we now believe holds even greater practical promise for refashioning education reform for the 21st century.

GRAHAM Leicester
DIRECTOR
INTERNATIONAL Futures Forum

Introduction

'The vision for Curriculum for Excellence is to achieve transformational change in Scottish education.'

Cabinet Secretary for Education and Lifelong Learning, Scotland, April 2008

EDUCATION is a key enabler of social, cultural and economic development for every nation in the 21st century. Improving education – especially for school-age young people – is a priority for governments across the world. Many, like the Scottish Government Minister quoted above, yearn for something more than 'improvement', aiming instead for nothing less than 'transformational change' in the education system to make it fit for today's fast-moving and boundlessly complex times.

Experience suggests they are likely to fail. One unavoidable lesson from numerous attempts at educational reform worldwide is that natural conservatism, vested interests, the enduring infrastructure of schools, the gold standard of individual written examinations and even market forces all conspire to bolster the status quo in the face of transformational intentions. We can expect incremental improvement at best.

This book argues that a better understanding of how transformative innovation happens combined with practical tools and policy support will improve on this poor record.

First, it is essential to acknowledge a distinction between incremental innovation, which merely sustains, improves or adjusts the existing system; and transformative innovation, which paves the way for something very different. Without that distinction education policy inevitably remains confined within the rich but ultimately limiting repertoire of set plays, to use a sporting analogy, based on maintenance and improvement of the status quo.

To move beyond incremental reform we have to learn how to introduce the new in the presence of the old in ways that do not result in innovation being captured and co-opted by the existing system to keep it going a little longer. This is a process not of revolution but of transition, built around actions carefully designed to ease entrenched systems towards visions of a different future. This can be done – but only if the forces that tug systems towards 'improvement' are fully recognised and if there are, at the very least, equal and opposite forces in the form of components of a shared vision of something different to draw people towards their higher aspirations.

The authors can speak with this degree of confidence because the insights, tools, suggestions and recommendations in the pages that follow are rooted firmly in practical experience. We start from the recognition that the Scottish Government's *Curriculum for Excellence*[2] is a new kind of permissive policy instrument and an invitation to transformational change in the education system. International Futures Forum (IFF) has been working, with others, in recent years to help realise that potential.

But this is not just a book about Scotland. We see Scotland's educational performance as typical of other nations. Scotland has been doing reasonably well in the international league tables, although there are questions about how well it serves either the strugglers or the high achievers. Yet we are becoming conscious that these international tables may no longer be evaluating the right competencies for the 21st century.[3] Further, for Scotland (like many developed economies) the era of rapid progress up the league table is ending and diminishing returns are setting in. Hence 'transformational change' is now on the agenda.

Over the past several years we have worked with a wide variety of educationalists, practitioners, policy makers and others in the Scottish education community to explore how this might be achieved. We have used the IFF three horizons framework to open up a strategic and visionary conversation about transforming education. We have followed that up with more detailed work exploring tensions and dilemmas between where we are today and where we would like to get to. We have developed a set of tools and support processes to move the conversation from vision to action. And we have outlined the shifts in the policy framework we think are necessary to create more space for the many 'pragmatic visionaries' we have found throughout the system who could become the pioneers of next practice.[4]

We believe this practical experience, and the results it is generating in Scotland, are widely applicable. Indeed, since the first edition of this book was published this transformative approach has attracted positive attention in different parts of the world – particularly the US, Asia and Australia. And international policy-makers are starting to look on with curiosity – if not envy – at the permissive policy framework set in Scotland by *Curriculum for Excellence*.

But the question remains: how can we make it work? How can government and other agencies best support a permissive programme of radical innovation in education? How can schools themselves take the lead?

This book explains how. It tells a story in six sections:

- a widespread international story of disappointment in educational reform
- the three horizons framework for thinking about longer-term transformational change
- the limitations of international models of 'standards-based reform'
- developing a transformative framework in Scotland
- an outline of the tools and processes that are shifting the Scottish system into the future
- recommendations for a policy framework to encourage transformative innovation in education: 'making shift happen'.

Education for a Changing World

Shift Happens

In August 2006 Karl Fisch, a high school teacher in Colorado, pulled together a set of data about the way the world is changing as a conversation starter for a staff faculty meeting. He called his presentation 'Did You Know – Shift Happens'. The presentation displayed a series of facts about the pace of change and the tectonic shifts in the world that are challenging many of our assumptions about the effectiveness of our education systems.

Fisch posted the presentation on his blog – the Fischbowl. It hit a nerve and quickly gained worldwide attention. Now it has been viewed online by more than 15 million people, and shown to countless more at conferences, workshops and presentations.[5]

Why? Because it is a powerful and simple representation of what we all know but find difficult to face up to. We live in powerful times. The world is changing. The future is radically uncertain. And the challenge for educators is daunting. As the presentation memorably puts it:

'We are currently preparing students for jobs that don't yet exist, using technologies that have not been invented, in order to solve problems we don't even know are problems yet.'

But Not in Education

Fisch's presentation is so powerful because we also sense how utterly out of step its message is with the pace of change in education systems worldwide. We see a pattern of steady, incremental improvement in education that continues to push the relevant statistics on participation and attainment ever higher, but a singular lack of transformative innovation.

School remains a perennial institution, maturing in Victorian times and little changed in its essence in centuries. The great expansion in education provision was driven by the needs of an industrialising economy. Today's economy and society have different needs. But while the factory whistle is now a museum piece, the school bell that imitates it remains a ubiquitous reminder of another age and children are still arranged in learning groups according to their date of manufacture.

The warning lights have been flashing red for decades now, but earnest efforts at improvement have failed to keep up with the changing world. The OECD in 2002 described an era of 'discontinuous change' in learning and education, 'revolution, not reform'. It has yet to transpire. The theme of the *European Journal of Education's* special volume on educational futures in 2007 was the gap between a growing understanding of the need for educational innovation and the persistence of disappointing practice. 'How come the more we know the less we use?' the editors asked.[6]

In spite of its upbeat title, McKinsey's 2010 report on 'How the world's most improved school systems keep getting better' told a sorry tale about education reform overall. 'Lots of energy, little light' was the headline summary. 'Most OECD countries tripled their spending on education in real terms between 1970 and 1994. Unfortunately, student outcomes in a large number of systems either stagnated or regressed.'[7]

The story of the last 25 years is perhaps most simply and powerfully told in relation to the United States – one of the most innovative nations on earth. In 1983 the National Commission on Excellence in Education published its landmark report *A Nation at Risk*. It spoke of a 'rising tide of mediocrity that threatens our very future as a nation and a people. What was unimaginable a generation ago has begun to occur - others are matching and surpassing our educational attainments'.

The response to this wake-up call was technical and managerial – improving the efficiency of the system, the quality of the inputs, managing the numbers. The results have been less than dramatic. There is the pain of the economist in this conclusion from the Heritage Foundation think tank in 1990:

> *'As a result of the past decade's efforts, classes have never been smaller and per-pupil spending and teacher salaries have never been higher -- and student performance has never been lower.'*

The pain of the politician is audible in US Education Secretary Rod Paige's lament in 2004:

> *'Is it too much to ask that a third-grade child read at a third-grade level?'*

And there is the pain of the entrepreneur looking to hire talent in Bill Gates' observation in 2005:

> *'American high schools are obsolete. Our high schools were designed 50 years ago to meet the needs of another age. Until we design them to meet the needs of the 21st century, we will keep limiting – even ruining – the lives of millions of Americans every year.'*

Reviewing the sorry saga Larry Cuban concludes:

> *'The surface is agitated and turbulent, while the ocean floor is calm and serene. Policy churns dramatically, creating the appearance of major changes while deep below the surface life goes on largely uninterrupted.'[8]*

Overall, across the developed world, governments have formulated new missions and aspirational targets for education, but none so far as we can tell has yet made the breakthrough to transformative practice. Educational system leaders are good at producing development programmes which are frenetic and burdensome to practitioners, incomprehensible and disruptive to both parents and learners but ultimately leave the essentials of the scene completely unaltered.

Resignation and fatalism are setting in. The debate is getting highly emotional and polarised. As critique of the existing system becomes more incendiary and revolutionary to provoke change, defence inevitably becomes more entrenched. Even the perennially hopeful Barack Obama is daunted when it comes to education:

> *'Our debate seems stuck between those who want to dismantle the system and those who would defend an indefensible status quo.'* [9]

The Dynamics of Long Term Change

How Shift Happens

It is helpful to step back and take a wider, more considered view of what is going on. What we are seeing in this story of education reform is a familiar pattern of change and resistance playing out over time.

For a number of years now IFF has been investigating the processes of longer-term societal change. We are impressed by former UK government policy adviser Geoff Mulgan's observation that governments tend to overestimate what they can achieve in the short term (and therefore become frustrated and disappointed) and underestimate what they can achieve in the longer term (and therefore pay it too little attention).

So how might we go about putting that insight into practice? How can policy be designed for both short-term encouragement and long-term effectiveness?

We have found a three horizons model of longer-term change a useful framework both for understanding the deeper processes of long-term societal change, and for designing more effective policy interventions.[10] We have used the model to prompt discussion of transformative innovation in a variety of settings - e.g. energy policy, healthcare, financial services, criminal justice. And education.

Transformative Innovation in Education

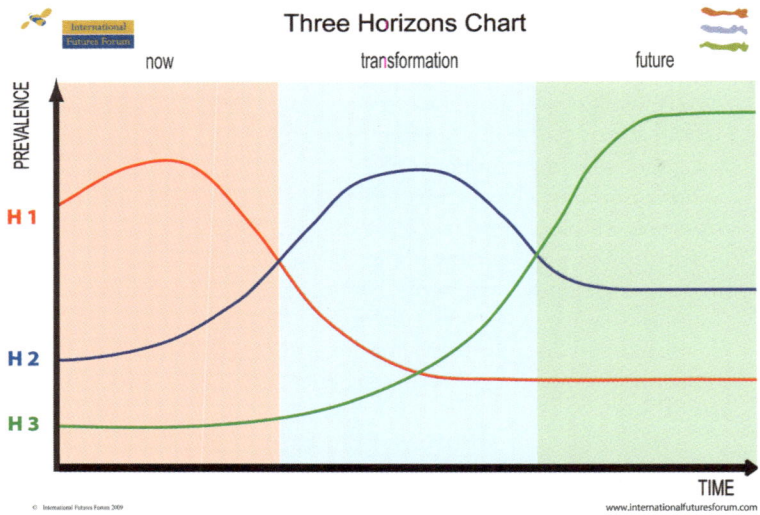

THREE horizons is a simple framework originally featured in *The Alchemy of Growth*.[11] It suggests that in order to sustain growth a company needs to think in terms of short-, medium- and longer-term time horizons, managing for current performance whilst also exploring future opportunities.

IFF has adapted the framework for use outside the business context. Rather than seeking present and future growth opportunities, we have adopted the framework of three horizons as a way of understanding long-term social change over time. The theoretical justification for such a reframing is set out by Curry and Hodgson in their article for the *Journal of Futures Studies*.[12] They point out, for example, that in the field of technology foresight, there comes a point in the future where the technology that might appear cannot be forecast simply by looking at what the market wants or what is in development in research labs. Some of what appears in the future will be the result of the imagination and desire of researchers pursuing their own aspirations and values today. This perspective gives each horizon, and the relationships between them, a rather different quality – as explained in more detail below.

The first horizon – H1 – is the dominant system at present. It represents 'business as usual'. As the world changes, so aspects of business as usual begin to feel out of place or no longer fit for purpose. In the end 'business as usual' is superseded by new ways of doing things.

Innovation has started already in light of the apparent shortcomings of the first horizon system. This forms a second horizon – H2. At some point the innovations become more effective than the original system. This is a point of disruption. Clayton Christensen called it the 'innovator's dilemma' – should you protect your mature business that is on the wane or invest in the innovation that looks as if it might replace it?

Meanwhile, there are other innovations happening already that today look way off beam. This is fringe activity. It feels like it is a long way from H1, based on fundamentally different premises. These are the first stirrings of a third horizon – H3. This horizon is the long-term successor to business as usual – the product of radical innovation that introduces a completely new way of doing things.

As an example we might see H1 as the mainframe computer. H2 as the desktop. H3 is mobile access to the cloud via the internet. Or, in terms of the school system, H1 might be universal mass education. H2 might be personalised education tailored around the student. H3 might be open access education – what I want, when I want, where I want – possibly without traditional schools at all.

All three horizons are always present. Aspects of H1 will persist in any new 'business as usual'. Aspects of H3 are always evident, if not obvious, in current discourse and argument and in all kinds of educational activity on the fringes of the dominant system. And H2, like a moving border between past and future, is all around us in examples of innovative alternative practice.

But the first horizon's commitment is to survival. The current system can maintain its dominance even in a changing world either by suppressing second and third horizon innovation, or by co-opting it to support the old system. These behaviours lead to variants on the smooth transition depicted above – notably the common 'capture and extend' scenario in which innovations in H2 are 'mainstreamed' in order to prolong the life of the existing system against the grain of a changing world.

The three horizons model offers a straightforward way into a conversation about:

- the dominant system and the challenges to its sustainability into the future, i.e. the case for change (H1)
- the desirable future state, the ideal system we desire and of which we can identify elements in the present that give us encouragement and inspiration (H3)
- the nature of the tensions and dilemmas between H3 vision and H1 reality, and the distinction between innovations that are essentially technical, incremental and adaptive serving to prolong the status quo and those that are transformative and help to bring the third horizon vision closer to reality (H2)
- developing a mature perspective that accepts the need *both* to address the challenges to the first horizon *and* nurture the seeds of the third. This is not an either/or, good/bad discussion. We need both to 'keep the lights on' today, and to find a way of keeping them on a generation from now in very different circumstances. Some call this maintaining 'safe running' during the process of change. We call it 'redesigning the plane whilst flying it'.

In the context of trying to find ways to stimulate new thinking about the future throughout the school system, we have found that the framework's principal virtue is that people find it simple and intuitive. The three modes of thinking that it encourages – managing the existing system, brainstorming promising innovation, and aspiring to something better in the future – are perfectly natural and can be heard in any day-to-day conversation.

But in a professional environment the voice of the third horizon is usually suppressed ('dream on!'), the voice of the second often dismissed ('that would never work here'), and the voice of the first is very rarely positive ('we're all going to hell in a handcart'). Explicitly framing the conversation in the three horizons framework legitimises all three voices in the conversation and shifts its character in the process.

Three Faces of Innovation

A further interesting dimension of the three horizons framework is the fresh insight it offers on the question of innovation. In practice in workshop settings people tend quickly to identify themselves with one or other of the horizons. The horizons are not only timelines but also mindsets.

The dominant mindset in H1 is managerial. It is about maintaining the system, improving its performance, maximising its potential. The dominant mindset in H2 is entrepreneurial. It is about seeing and grasping opportunities that the changing landscape offers. The dominant mindset in H3 is visionary and aspirational. It is about standing for something, a values-based position. H3 practice in the present is down to people who choose to operate and advocate in a certain way because they believe it to be right, whatever the rest of the world thinks.

None of these mindsets is wrong. In the process of change all three horizons will always be present. Indeed, as President Obama's observation (above) suggests, much of our frustration with ineffective change efforts to date may be down to the fact that we tend to polarise into defendants of H1 and advocates for an 'unrealistic' H3 - without paying sufficient attention to the subtle processes in H2 that might enable the transition.

These different mindsets also reveal three faces of innovation. Innovation in H1 is for efficiency. It is about improvement, getting the most out of the existing system. This is the mode brought to prominence, for example, by the success of the British Olympic cycling team – the 'aggregation of marginal gains' in order to achieve excellence. In a changing world it has variously been described as 'maintaining', 'sustaining', 'adjusting' or 'improving' innovation.

Innovation in H2 is about seeing and seizing opportunity. Different ideas are conceived, tried and tested. Some work, others fail. But what is the selection mechanism? In practice, in the absence of any other frame of reference, innovations stand or fall in H2 depending on their capacity to support and appeal to H1. Business as usual, after all, holds most of the power and resource and takes the critical decisions about research funding, about purchasing, and about policy.

So, in practice, innovations in H2 have a tendency to look backwards. Most of them are conceived in those terms – designed to fix the existing system in H1. Others just happen to 'catch on' – but again largely because they succeed in fixing or improving the old system, prolonging its life. Where something takes off at scale in business it has caught the mass market – the holy grail for much innovation. In policy circles this same process of being taken up enthusiastically by the existing system is called 'mainstreaming' – and is likewise the unexamined goal of most would-be reformers.

But what if the goals of H1 are unsustainable? What if there is more to modern life than getting to the finish line in the velodrome faster than ever before? Innovation in H3 is about opening up a strategic conversation about the way the world is changing that allows us to re-examine the unstated

The Dynamics of Long Term Change

assumptions of H1, including what constitutes 'success' or 'excellence' or 'value'.[13] This is essentially a public duty and therefore a central role for government and public servants.[14]

H3 is the dimension in which we can talk about 'the jobs that don't yet exist using technologies not yet invented to solve problems we don't even know are problems'. Without this perspective all innovation in H2 is likely to be drawn towards improving the status quo.

With an active vision and imagination about the nature of the third horizon we open up another possibility. We can design innovations that work to shift the existing system towards something radically different. Such innovations help create the conditions for the eventual realisation of H3 aspirations. It is this form of innovation that is desperately needed in education.

The Limitations of 'Standards-based Reform'

Shifting Education

The three horizons framework highlights the tenacity of ever-present incumbent systems that argue powerfully for their survival. That is especially true in education.

The institution of school is strong and has become an enduring part of the infrastructure of many people's lives. That has tended to breed a reluctance to experiment. There is also a natural bias in education systems towards conserving the past. We tend to pass on the wisdom of our own generation to the next. That sets up an inevitable learning lag. As adults we want the best for our children and tend to use our own education as our main reference point – justifying both a natural conservatism ('it was good enough for me') and a focus on managerial improvements in the existing system ('my education was OK, but I want better for my children').

The demand for 'improvement' and 'excellence' within the existing H1 system has fed the search for standard measures and objectivity in order to make comparisons between providers. Increasingly these measures have become international, designed to benchmark the performance of whole education systems: the Programme for International Student Assessment (PISA), for example, the Progress in International Reading Literacy Study (PIRLS), the Trends in International Mathematics and Science Study (TIMSS).

These measures have become part of the institutional infrastructure, the universal context within which education systems operate and the benchmark against which 'successful innovations' are inevitably measured. Every education ministry in the world now effectively has the same policy objective: to raise its standing in the international league tables. The international system has locked in on a single model. And we are all consequently investing more in trying to shorten the long tail of underachievement (a task for which it was not designed) than in raising the bar for those already ticking the PISA boxes.

The Limitations of 'Standards-based Reform'

Four Box Model: Standards-Based Systemic Reform		
Have Resources	Show and Tell – help them learn from best practice	Exemplars – spread the word
Don't Have Resources	'Failing School' – take it over	Ready to Improve – fund them
	Don't Know What To Do	Know What To Do

The dominant approach is captured in the neat four-box model of so-called 'standards-based systemic reform' illustrated above.[15] It describes the four modes of government policy intervention available for schools that either have or don't have resources and either do or don't know how to 'improve'. This is the limited but highly influential playbook of H1 'innovation' – how to get the best out of the existing system.

At the time it became influential in policy circles, in the US in the early 1990s, this approach offered hope that systematic central policy direction could arrest a chaotic decline in some parts of the education system by introducing minimum standards and managerial discipline for continuous improvement. Its spirit can be seen in the implicit emphasis on minimum standards in the 'No Child Left Behind' programme.

However, as one of the architects of the movement in the US (Mike Smith) has acknowledged, 'the theory and practice of standards-based reform does not directly address the issues of stimulating innovation within the public system, or of safety valves for parents and students who would like an alternative to standard public schools.' In other words, H1 innovation for efficiency gains and assured minimum standards may be necessary but it is certainly not sufficient.

Part of the limitation of standards-based reform is that it relies on universal 'standards' that may themselves be of questionable value as the world changes. The OECD's 'Definition and Selection of Key Competencies' study was a brave, multi-disciplinary, multi-national five year attempt to question whether the multitude of international league tables are actually any longer measuring the kinds of competencies we will need in the 21st century.[16] The depressing conclusion was that they are not – but since competencies better suited to the needs of the 21st century are not easily assessed with single indicators, still less on any objective scale across countries and cultures for the sake of international comparison, we will just have to go on measuring the wrong things as a misleading proxy for measuring the right ones.[17]

It is not only school systems that stick to what they know, even in the face of evidence they are not fit for purpose. June Delano's research on US executive education is striking.[18] When business leaders are asked about the key factors explaining their current success, i.e. how they learn, nearly half mention challenging assignments (learning on the job), some 20% mention either mentors, significant others or learning through hardships, and only 7% mention learning in the classroom. Yet it is learning in the classroom that still dominates this $10bn a year industry in the US. Why are so many smart, money-aware people pouring such a huge resource into an activity of such questionable value?

The Limitations of 'Standards-based Reform'

Delano's answers to that question refer specifically to executive education, but they might be generalised for any education system as possible factors standing in the way of moving beyond the first horizon. They are:

- the underlying philosophy: industrial age, economies of scale, etc.
- the infrastructure of the teaching industry: schools, universities, staff, heavy sunk costs
- parents'/purchasers' expectations: 'it was good enough for me', straightforward, familiar outcome measurements
- teaching professionals: steeped in familiar methods, 'the wrong people for the new task'.

In Scotland we carry the further burden of international admiration for our education system. That is a dubious honour. It can reinforce complacency – as do Scotland's PISA ratings. And whilst there is a lively community of H2 innovators, networking, sharing and meeting on- and offline, sooner or later they inevitably hit the glass ceiling of H1 norms and expectations. The challenge is always to achieve scale – and typically first horizon systems and policy frameworks will interpret that as 'more of the same, but better'.

Transforming Education: Scotland Case Study

Scotland's Opportunity

THE pull of the dominant, business-as-usual H1 systems in education is clearly immensely powerful. The three horizons framework gives us a way to acknowledge that power without being entirely subsumed by it. It allows us to think carefully about the central challenge of innovation designed to shift the system to a new state rather than simply fix or improve it: the challenge of introducing the new in the presence of the old.

Scotland provides an excellent setting in which to explore this approach. Successive Scottish Governments have voiced a desire to transform the education system. The present chosen vehicle – *Curriculum for Excellence* – may constitute the kind of enabling policy instrument that such an intention requires. But it will take more than good intentions for this reform effort to deliver where so many others have failed.

The following pages describe IFF's work in support of *Curriculum for Excellence* and what we have learned as a result about moving an education system beyond incremental improvement.

We start with a description of the central policy instrument. We next locate this in a wider context – a 'strategic conversation' about education in Scotland. That reveals the nature of the journey Scottish education needs to make and the landscape it will have to navigate in order to make the transition.

This leads to the final sections of the book: these look at how government can actively support a process of 'transformative innovation' and how, suitably supported, schools themselves can take a lead.

Curriculum for Excellence

THE roots of *Curriculum for Excellence* lie in a national debate on the state of school education launched by the Scottish Government in 2002. Much of that debate centred on an outdated curriculum: how could it become less cluttered, more relevant, more fun, more flexible between academic and vocational pathways? Ministers duly established a Curriculum Review Group which in November 2004 published *A Curriculum for Excellence*.

The Curriculum Review Group report provides an explicit statement of the purposes of education in Scotland – to enable young people to become 'successful learners, confident individuals, responsible citizens and effective contributors'. It also sets out several principles for curriculum design – challenge and enjoyment, breadth, progression, depth, personalisation and choice, coherence and relevance. The overall goal of the *Curriculum for Excellence* programme is to achieve translation of the four purposes into practice.

This is an ambitious goal which will not be realised overnight. As the official literature says:

> *'The intention is to alter the balance between a process that is heavily dependent on content, and learning and teaching approaches that improve pupils' understanding of what is being taught. This is not a one-off change but the start of a continuous process of review to ensure that the curriculum remains up to date.'*

Curriculum for Excellence has become the principal guide to the process of 'national reform' in Scotland's education system and is now supported by a plethora of further documents and other mechanisms dealing with aspects of its full realisation.

One of the most remarkable things about this policy framework is the near unanimity of the authors and the almost universal welcome it received, particularly from the teaching profession, when it was published. The positive reason for this is that it is a succinct and strong restatement of the vision and values of the education system.

The other reason may not be so positive: it is written at a high level of generality so people could sign up to it while holding very different interpretations of what it meant. The sharpest division has always been between those who see it as the next in a long line of initiatives for incremental reform, moving forward from the status quo in a well organised and systematic way, and those who see it as a much longer-term, visionary document where the destination, however fuzzy in outline, is more important than the route.

This is a critical distinction. It is possible to see *Curriculum for Excellence* as a reform programme like any other, another version of the four-box H1 set of prescriptions examined earlier (see page 23). Those schools in Scotland ostensibly waiting for additional funding, or for more detailed 'guidance', have probably interpreted it in that way. And the official machinery turning out documentation, learning outcomes and experiences, timelines and tick-box schedules in response may well be geared towards that interpretation.

But there is another way of thinking about *Curriculum for Excellence*: take it at face value. Understand that it is an enabling document – setting out broad principles, values, purposes and outcomes that have an impeccable international pedigree. The UNESCO Commission on Education in the 21st Century advocates a very similar set of core purposes – learning to be, to do, to know and to live together – which have also been picked up in other jurisdictions.

Seen in this way, it becomes a new kind of policy instrument. It potentially provides what pragmatic visionaries in education have been wanting for so long: a permissive policy framework that will encourage the transition of a mature system into new forms more appropriate for the times... and encourage this to happen not through a process of top-down direction, but through a process of supported professional learning.

It is this orientation that IFF has chosen to explore, working with professionals, practitioners and national agencies in Scotland and elsewhere. We see this as an opportunity to move beyond the failed mantra of 'standards-based reform' and into more transformative territory.

Enabling the Strategic Conversation

IN January 2007 IFF convened an exploratory workshop to address the prospects for *Curriculum for Excellence* as a prompt for effective educational reform. The workshop sought to provide both a space and a framework (the three horizons model) for an open, honest, strategic conversation.

The event generated a rich picture of the emerging policy landscape around the 'delivery' and future prospects for the set of ideas that is *Curriculum for Excellence*. Participants were also impressed by the way the three horizons framework had opened up the conversation and suggested that it might be valuable in other settings: teacher education, professional development activities, strategic thinking and planning in education authorities, individual schools, other services.

Thus encouraged, we began to use the framework to stimulate a richer than usual conversation about innovation in a variety of other settings:

- with a group of educators in the city of Dundee, focusing on the personalisation agenda
- with an international group of educators in a workshop on educational leadership held in York District, Ontario
- with a local education authority in England as part of its work on professional learning for strategic leadership

- with a group of school leaders as part of their professional learning through an international study visit
- with a group of senior school Inspectors in Scotland focusing on how to make the transition from H1 towards H3.

These were all valuable experiences, and each helped to flesh out our picture of the emerging landscape – challenges in the present, visions of the future, and promising innovations that might lead from one to the other. It was striking to find so many educators, teachers and administrators happily visioning a future in which their own institutions – schools – might no longer exist. That has the mark of transformative thinking.

The Emerging Landscape of Education in Scotland

FOLLOWING these varied and encouraging experiences, IFF re-convened a number of the participants from the original workshop plus other interested parties intrigued by developments over the course of the year.

We had discovered that the three horizons framework is a very effective and intuitive way of opening up a broader strategic conversation, and introduces the element of third horizon vision without which 'innovation' will almost inevitably slip backwards towards improving the status quo. We had further discovered an enthusiasm and willingness to regard *Curriculum for Excellence* as a new kind of policy instrument, explicitly enabling the journey towards the third horizon – for those equipped to think through the implications.

What we had also uncovered was an emergent picture of the three horizons of Scottish education. Our inquiries suggested a current system (H1) dominated by an institutional infrastructure already perhaps twenty years past its sell-by date, held in place by a native conservatism, an unwillingness to 'experiment' with children's education and the general levels of stress involved in just keeping the whole show on the road.

There is also a vision of the future (H3), just like the one expressed implicitly in *Curriculum for Excellence*: of dedicated, creative, reflective professionals, distributed leadership, preparing young people for the unknown and to live 'fulfilled lives in a well-functioning society' (to quote the OECD DeSeCo study).

And there are also signs of encouragement (H2) that we are capable of making the transition – although many of the innovations identified are not directly related to *Curriculum for Excellence* and tend to be adopted more enthusiastically at primary school than at secondary school level (such as multi-faceted exploration of issues rather than subject-based teaching; or the 'assessment for learning' philosophy that originated in the work of Paul Black and Dylan Wiliam at the London Institute of Education as a more empowering form of keeping track of pupils' progress).

Tensions in the Transition Zone

ALTHOUGH generated in Scotland and apparently a description of the Scottish education system, this is a recognisably generic picture of three horizons of education throughout the developed world.

The next phase of our work therefore sought to explore more directly the kinds of support that government and others might most usefully provide for those seeking to manage the transition more successfully from H1 practice to a very different H3 vision.

It is clear that the challenge lies in the transition zone. This is a risky space. It can be chaotic and confusing with so many different ideas competing for attention. And it can feel an uncomfortable and under-valued place for many professionals.

It is H1 after all that hires, promotes and rewards performance. It is H1 measures that determine success and career advancement. There is some prestige to be gained in H3 as well – we still put aside a little time for visioning sessions, awaydays, 'blue skies' thinking. There are reputations to be made in that space.

But H2 is often the Cinderella zone for leaders in all sectors. This is not the enticing realm of the imagination. It is the realm of real work, practical action. It has to struggle for resource from H1 and is inevitably judged – usually far too soon – by the same standards as existing mature H1 systems. And plenty of innovations fail.

The transition zone is also inevitably characterised by tensions – between the power of the first horizon and the attraction of the third. To navigate the transition effectively we must understand these tensions, and why they persist. There are elements of the first horizon system that work well and that we are reluctant to abandon, yet they are at odds with elements of a third horizon vision that we suspect will better serve the future. This is why it is so difficult to introduce the new in the presence of the old.

We can observe many such tensions in the landscape today. Doubtless others could add more from their own experience. The important thing for effective innovation is to acknowledge up front that they exist – that this is the nature of the real policy landscape we are required to navigate. Here are some examples from our reading of the Scottish landscape, likely echoed in systems around the world:

Attraction of H1		Attraction of H3
Stability/Predictability	↔	Uncertainty, dynamism, excitement
Fixed infrastructure	↔	Flexible, creative spaces
System running at maximum	↔	Redundancy for learning and innovation, time and space for regeneration
School as setting for cutting-edge education	↔	Life as setting for cutting-edge education
Discipline and mass scale	↔	Love and human scale
Political control, equity	↔	Self-organisation, possibility
Clear measures of success (biased towards under-achiever?)	↔	Emergent measures of success
Short-term evidence (crops)	↔	Long-term evidence (trees)
Evidence-based policy	↔	Inspiring stories of transformational practice

Ostrich or Eagle? Dealing with Dilemmas

TYPICALLY in looking at these kinds of lists we think either/or. We plump for one side of the polarity or the other. We might even take a vote. But where there is a genuine tension, where both sides of the polarity have value, that will not do. We need to think both/and. That requires a less familiar style of thinking – wrestling with dilemmas.

This kind of thinking was pioneered by the management theorist Charles Hampden-Turner. He started to place the tensions not at different ends of a spectrum but orthogonally at right angles – thus creating a dilemma space with a sweet spot (top right corner) in which you can combine the best of *both* values. In the dilemma resolution space you can have your cake and eat it.

Thus if we think of H1 and H3 as value sets it becomes clearer that effective educational reform is not simply about ridding ourselves of the first horizon system. It still has a role to play in the future, just not such a dominant one. If we insist on thinking of H3 replacing H1 rather than finding a new creative and generative synergy with H1 then it is not surprising it is so difficult to make the transition. Effective strategy and policy needs to confront the dilemmas in the transition zone rather than evade or succumb to them.

Hampden-Turner found that most dilemmas take a similar form. There is generally a 'rock value' with the quality of the immovable object on one horn, and a 'whirlpool value' with the quality of an irresistible force on the other. And if you cling exclusively to either then the other will find a way back in to get you eventually.

VERTICAL "HARD" VALUE
The Rock
"the immovable object"

HORIZONTAL "SOFT" VALUE
The Whirlpool
"the irresistible force"

Hampden-Turner was also a systems thinker and understood that underneath this structure is a cybernetic system. Moving towards the resolution space in the top right hand corner, where 1 + 1 = 3, is not a simple linear process.

Instead it is like tacking a sailing boat against the wind – where the wind is blowing you on to the rocks of the first horizon. You may need to move towards the rock value for a while, before turning to introduce more of the whirlpool value. We call this 'the dilemma dance'. It represents the smart H2 policy course – in which H2 innovations are introduced and eventually start to cohere into the new H3 system.

There are five possible outcomes in performing the dilemma dance. If you stick to the rock value you become a dinosaur and die out. If you stick to the whirlpool value you become a unicorn – a mythical beast. If you compromise you end up as an ostrich, head in the sand. If you get stuck in the zone of conflict you end up as Dr Doolittle's push-me-pull-you. But if you get to the resolution space you soar like an eagle.

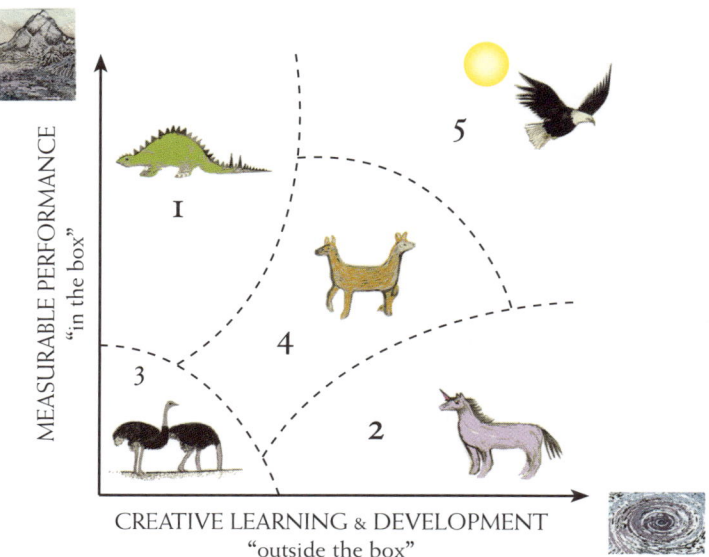

Transformative Innovation in Education

Exploring the Dilemmas of the Second Horizon

To illustrate this approach, it is instructive to take a worked example. One of the tensions already identified in our work in Scotland is between the desire for quality assurance and standards on the one hand and for freedom of choice and diverse transformative innovation on the other.

It is tempting to polarise this as a struggle between the interests of the public assurance role of national agencies on the one hand and innovators, pupils, teachers and parents on the other. But in practice we can tell that this is a real dilemma because it is possible to see this tension experienced acutely *within* the schools Inspectorate – whose task, after all, is both to *inspect* the existing system and *inspire* innovation towards next practice. Indeed, the new national agency Education Scotland, established in July 2011, is working on approaches that can meet both of these core objectives.

To work through this example, treating a tension as a dilemma rather than a simple choice, we can divide the dilemma space into five sections, corresponding to the zones shown in the graphic above. Then for the tension in question we can perform the following step-by-step analysis, working through the zones in order:

- Zone 1: State the primary value which is solid and unshakeable embodied in the current H1 system
- Zone 2: State the core value that must be central to the new H3 system
- Zone 3: Identify some of the typical compromises that sweep the tension between these values under the carpet
- Zone 4: Characterise the tensions that can break out into conflicts between the rock and the whirlpool
- Zone 5: Seek creative resolution:
  a) What can the rock offer the whirlpool without compromise?

b) What can the whirlpool offer the rock without compromise?

The template overleaf shows the kinds of issues and contributions that arise in discussing the dilemma between control and standards (the rock) and freedom of choice and diversity of innovation (the whirlpool) working through the sequence above. The content is purely illustrative – to give a sense of how to use the dilemma template in practice.

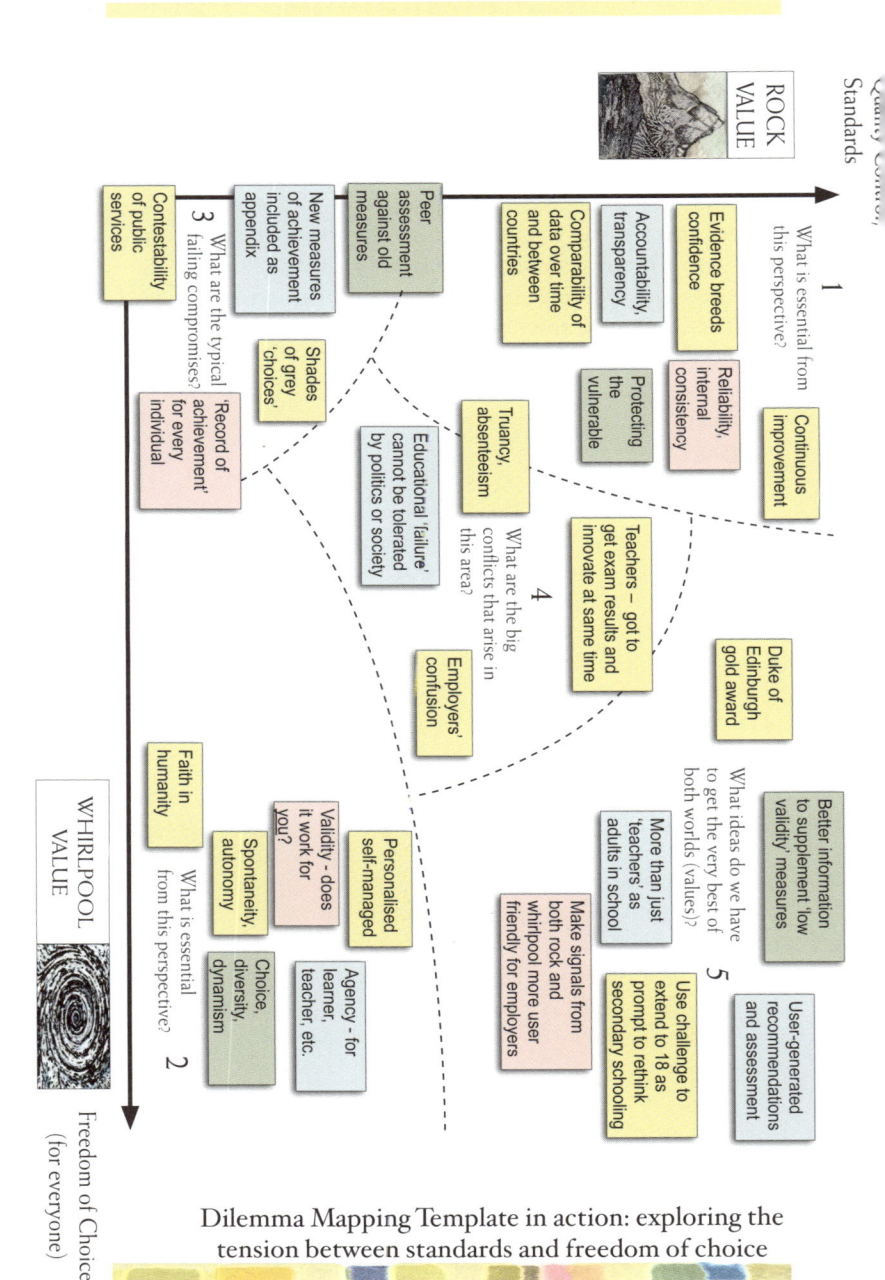

Transformative Innovation in Education

ROCK VALUE — Quality Control, Standards

1 What is essential from this perspective?

- Peer assessment against old measures
- New measures of achievement included as appendix
- Comparability of data over time and between countries
- Accountability, transparency
- Evidence breeds confidence
- Reliability, internal consistency
- Protecting the vulnerable
- Continuous improvement
- Shades of grey 'choices'
- Truancy, absenteeism
- Educational 'failure' cannot be tolerated by politics or society
- 'Record of achievement' for every individual
- Contestability of public services

3 What are the typical failing compromises?

4 What are the big conflicts that arise in this area?

- Teachers – got to get exam results and innovate at same time
- Employers' confusion
- Duke of Edinburgh gold award

WHIRLPOOL VALUE — Freedom of Choice (for everyone)

2 What is essential from this perspective?

- Faith in humanity
- Validity - does it work for you?
- Spontaneity, autonomy
- Personalised self-managed
- Choice, diversity, dynamism
- Agency - for learner, teacher, etc.

5 What ideas do we have to get the very best of both worlds (values)?

- Better information to supplement 'low validity' measures
- More than just 'teachers' as adults in school
- Make signals from both rock and whirlpool more user friendly for employers
- Use challenge to extend to 18 as prompt to rethink secondary schooling
- User-generated recommendations and assessment

Dilemma Mapping Template in action: exploring the tension between standards and freedom of choice

The 'rock' values are the good things that quality control delivers: consistency, transparency, reliability, protection against the system falling below a minimum standard, possibilities for consistent comparison of performance across time and between countries, the possibility of continuous improvement, etc.

The 'whirlpool' values supported by freedom of choice are about choice, diversity, dynamism, range of possibilities, spontaneity, autonomy, intelligent consumption, personal validity as a measure of usefulness, and a faith in humanity's capacity to make right choices for ourselves.

One route to the resolution space is to consider the present sites of conflict (zone 4). Who is experiencing conflict in the midst of this dilemma? Employers who want qualifications and soft skills and have lost faith in the measurement and assessment of both; truants and the community of disaffected youth whom school is failing and has failed for life; and teachers having to run the old system whilst innovating the new.

Combining the best of both values and seeking to address these existing sites of conflict brought this particular discussion to suggest new kinds of evaluation involving peer assessment and user-generated pooling of recommendations – commonplace as a practice now with web 2.0 social media sites. There could be better signalling and user-friendly information for employers both about existing qualifications and other skills and achievements. A choice of mentors in schools, as well as teachers, might be a way to marry the presence of both value sets.

The Duke of Edinburgh Gold Award, in which teams acquire new skills by undertaking community service, athletic and other tasks and also complete an outdoor expedition, looks like a good candidate for eagle status. It offers a certificate of quality that is recognised and valued by employers and others yet which is not based on a written examination, is experiential, team-based, and not delivered in the classroom. Inevitably the price we will pay for assessing what matters in this way is lower standards of reliability and comparability than can be achieved by measuring factual recall. This we believe is a price worth paying. Having that more widely accepted will need more extensive public debate. The growing status of the Duke of Edinburgh Award and other similar awards in the UK is a good sign.

This is one illustration of how to explore a tension as a dilemma. We could equally pursue the analysis with other examples – either of underlying tension between the present and the future or of conflict within the existing system. What the exercise quickly brings out in either case is the following:

- It is very easy to identify compromise solutions that suppress the tension without addressing it (zone 3). It is much more difficult to get to the resolution space (zone 5).
- A willingness to wrestle with and ride the horns of the dilemma in zone 4 prevents the slip into easy compromise, or the tendency to migrate to either pole of the discussion (seeing quality control and freedom of choice as potentially complementary rather than opposed values).
- It is interesting to find that wrestling with the dilemma and seeking creative ways to combine the best of both worlds often identifies existing practice that can now be seen in a new light – as exemplifying the third horizon in the present. As the science fiction author William Gibson remarked, 'the future is already here, just unevenly distributed'. But we first have to know what we are looking for.

Practical Approaches To Transformation

From Insight To Action

OUR analysis suggests that school systems the world over today face a dual challenge: first to envisage what is required of them in a changing world; second to translate that vision into effective practice. And the second challenge can seem at least as daunting as the first.

We in IFF have faced the same challenge in taking forward the work described in this book. We have found through experience that the three horizons framework is very effective at opening up a rich conversation about change in schools and, in particular, radical innovation that shifts well beyond the status quo. But the question remains: how to embed this thinking more widely within the education system? And, even more so, how to ensure that it results in action?

Clearly what is needed is a simple, practical approach that might bed down within existing school management structures and yet encourage the kind of transformative innovation that is now necessary. We can now say with confidence that we have developed exactly that – thanks to a close collaboration with Her Majesty's Inspectorate of Schools in Scotland.

We discovered in the course of our explorations that the Inspectorate shares an interest in how to move beyond incremental improvement in schools. To that end it had determined to add a 'forward look' to its other assessment processes. This would complement the existing 'inward look' (self-evaluation using data, professional judgements and stakeholder perceptions) and 'outward look' (benchmarking and learning from research and professional networks), by placing the school in the context of a changing world and an emerging and uncertain future. It hoped that adding a forward look would prompt the kinds of radical innovation it believes to be necessary to meet both the challenges and the promise of today's world.

Three Horizons Kit

WE decided that the three horizons framework was ideally suited to the forward look. Inspectors had experienced the framework themselves and enjoyed the depth and range of the conversations it had prompted. They suggested it would be good to encourage this kind of strategic conversation in all school leadership teams as part of the school improvement planning process.

Together we collaborated on the design of a simple Kit that would enable school senior teams to have the kind of wide-ranging three horizons conversations we had enjoyed. Under the title 'Opening Up Transformative Innovation', the Kit is now being made available to every school in Scotland.

Three Horizons Strategic Thinking Kit

The Kit is based around a set of cards to prompt a strategic conversation about the present and the future. On the cards are a set of statements about the changing world,

Practical Approaches To Transformation

about changing education policy and practice and about changing young people (three suits). Every statement on the cards is evidence-based, relating to something already happening, at some scale, somewhere in the world. This is a way of bringing current educational research and other knowledge into the process – getting the future into the conversation about school improvement.

The statements are then used to prompt a discussion (e.g. led by the headteacher, with senior staff, around the staffroom table) that is recorded, on post-it notes, on a three horizons chart (see page 16) against the two axes of prevalence and time. Senior students with experience of the Kit have themselves subsequently led such a process. Each card statement prompts at least two reflections to get the conversation going: is what is referred to on the card happening already or might it happen in the future? Is it a worrying sign of the existing system failing (H1) or a desirable feature for the future (H3)? The conversation flows from there.

With the addition of a die (to choose which 'suit' of cards to play), an egg timer to regulate play if necessary and a simple set of instructions to read and communicate to the other 'players', any group leader (often the headteacher) can manage a strategic conversation that in a couple of hours (or less) helps the team to populate their own three horizons landscape.

At this point groups – and headteachers – typically ask how to interpret the landscape they have discovered, and in particular how to incorporate the insights from their strategic conversation into a school improvement plan. Again working with the Inspectorate, testing and amending as we went, we developed a supplemental chart and a new set of instructions, now incorporated in the three horizons Kit, to process the three horizons conversation and to draw out its implications for a programme of innovation.

Transformative Innovation in Education

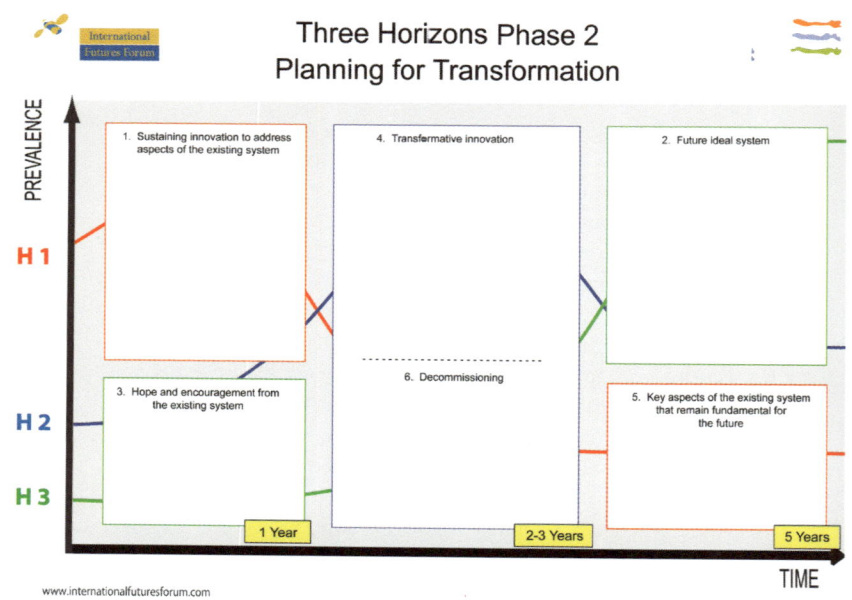

**Three Horizons Phase 2
Planning for Transformation**

- PREVALENCE (y-axis)
- TIME (x-axis): 1 Year, 2-3 Years, 5 Years
- H1, H2, H3

1. Sustaining innovation to address aspects of the existing system
2. Future ideal system
3. Hope and encouragement from the existing system
4. Transformative innovation
5. Key aspects of the existing system that remain fundamental for the future
6. Decommissioning

www.internationalfuturesforum.com

This second phase (see above) encourages the group to identify and to embellish from their earlier conversation both a vision for the future and features of the present system that suggest the vision can be achieved (box 3 on the chart above). In other words, they elaborate on the H3 ideal that they have identified and examples of it they know of in the present (anywhere in the world). Then they draw up an innovation portfolio consisting of three kinds of action:

- sustaining innovations required to address concerns about the existing system in order to keep it running (e.g. efficiency savings)
- aspects of the existing system that have no place in their imagined ideal future and therefore need to be gradually 'decommissioned'
- transformative innovation that will pave the way for their H3 vision.

Practical Approaches To Transformation

The instructions also seek to remove some of the fear that surrounds actually embarking on transformative innovation by suggesting that such action does not need to be daunting. As the instructions say, the action should be:

- small scale
- inspiring, to at least two or preferably three members of staff willing to support one another in giving it a go (i.e. avoid 'solo climbers')
- able to release resources from the first horizon system and direct them towards the third horizon (i.e. not require large, additional, up-front investment)
- capable of authentically illustrating the big picture developed in the earlier strategic conversation by helping to create a transition pathway towards the vision in the third horizon rather than simply improving the present system
- viral in nature in that others will adopt it because it works and not because it is imposed in a top-down manner.

Getting Into Action

WHAT these conversations in turn begin to reveal is a latent energy for radical innovation in most schools and always one or two individuals keen to try something different – to push the boundaries of their existing practice towards a desirable third horizon. Yet at the same time such schools also echo the Inspectorate's initial misgivings about implementation. With no substantial leadership experience or support, no time, no money, no training budget, no consultants or facilitators available, how can these groups of teachers take the next step: the move from insight to action?

Bearing in mind the Inspectorate's desire to shift its own role away from monitoring towards supporting and inspiring change, IFF decided at this point to train a number of inspectors in a set of simple but powerful tools to support people through change designed by our IFF colleague Jim Ewing.

These tools dovetail beautifully with the three horizons framework. Once a group has its three horizon mapping in place, once it has scoped the territory, making headway requires individuals to absorb the implications and to develop the courage to make a first step into the unknown towards the third horizon. Equally they need to do so with discipline and with a plan that is rooted in the challenges of the real world, not the fantasy world of magical thinking.

Ewing's tools are designed to work with this reality. He understands that if people are going to embark on genuine transformative innovation they will have to brave the uncertainty of having one foot in known reality while pushing off with the other into the unknown, secure in the belief that the next footing will materialise just in time. This requires us to develop the skills to listen for and engage the voices of resistance and avoidance, the statements of possibility and experiment, and the pragmatic targets and investments and disciplines necessary to bring our aspirations to fruition.

All three of these perspectives, like the three horizons, will be present in the conversation about taking an initiative to change the system: it is important to listen to and work with them all. That is particularly important for the voice of resistance – the naysayers and the cynics. It is important to include their energy in the conversation: it is extraordinary how potent a resource for change such people can become when they are really heard.

That requires conversational frameworks to handle the many contradictory emotions, anecdotes, facts and perspectives on the present and the future that will arise. It needs a process that does not dismiss the outworn but exhausts it, and thus enables the lateral, cross-current collisions of ideas which spawn a genuinely transformative approach. In other words, we need some additional hardware

Practical Approaches To Transformation

and software to move from the visionary constructs of H3 into committed and disciplined action.

Once the three horizons mapping is in place any group committed to action needs to (in no particular order):

- get to a practical belief or faith that it really can reshape the future
- create useful choices which transcend dilemmas and design optimal moves to make immediate dents in the universe, beginning now
- minimise wasted time, resources and angst as it brings its members and other needed resources into its work
- construct a scorecard of metrics of progress, stated in terms accepted and workable in the dominant H1 culture.

With Jim Ewing's help we introduced the Schools Inspectorate in Scotland to a suite of three tools that help a group to establish these necessary prerequisites for change. They are Impacto – a process for developing a coherent story about an initiative to enrol others; TransforMAP – a framework for understanding the process of change and, more importantly, resistance to change in individuals; and Implemento – a technique for planning an initiative that may feel daunting, to incorporate hindsight into the design in order to ward off disaster. These three approaches are described in a little more detail below (and now form part of the 'Tools for Transformative Innovation' included in the three horizons Kit for those who want to move beyond the strategic conversation and into effective action).

Impacto: The three horizons mapping provides the material for a story of transformation, a journey from the safety of H1 towards the aspirations of H3. We need to be able to communicate that story convincingly for ourselves, and to enrol others. Impacto provides a series of questions and a structure to draw out this story – about a group's inspiration, its plan, its purposes, the path it intends to follow and the commitments it is making.

This story can then be used to engage and enrol others – the board of governors, educational authority officers, other staff, parents, pupils and the wider community. The process is reflexive, adapting as necessary in response to these communications encounters and to the progress of the project itself. The Impacto story provides a reference to revisit and rebuild as things go along, both for the group and the wider community. It is a self-marketing case for change.

TransforMAP: This is a framework to help people articulate and understand their thoughts, feelings and urges to action (or inaction) as they go through the process of change. We all tend to use certain distinct language, frameworks of thinking and behaviours when we are working through transitional or uncertain times. We might show up as dark, light, fanciful, hopeful, fatalistic, open, uncertain, disciplined, directed, lost, and all at once! The TransforMAP makes operational sense of this cacophony which can otherwise bring a group to a confused halt as it encounters the ground moving under its feet.

The Map organises these thoughts, feelings and actions into 'voices' which we can listen for and converse with in ourselves and others. There is a voice of endings, a voice of reinvention, and a voice of realisation. Learning to listen to each other and transparently reflect what we hear helps to complete the expression of all three voices. These completions move everyone along through the process of change, minimising wasted resources and time, and – more importantly – the emotional angst that so often accompanies giving up the old for something uncertain and new.

Implemento: In articulating the three horizons landscape, the lure of the third horizon is a call to action. But what kind of action? Implemento provides a framework for playing out a variety of scenarios through a very wide range of possible outcomes – positive and negative –

Practical Approaches To Transformation

resulting from our actions. Looking for the emergent patterns across these outcomes reveals smarter initiatives and the real reasons to take them; initiatives which can be taken immediately to avoid wasted time and trouble and best assure positive movement in the direction of our aspirations.

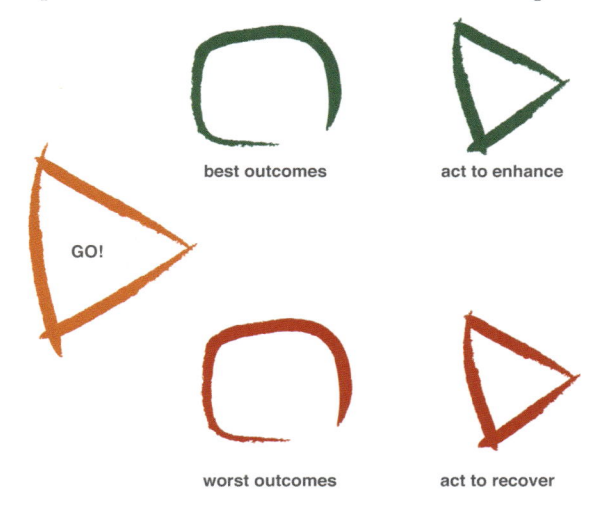

	best outcomes	act to enhance
GO!	worst outcomes	act to recover

Simplified Implemento

The process starts from our best guess for an initiative we think might work. The conversation plays that initiative out against the reality of the dilemma-strewn landscape of the H2 transition zone. One result is a balanced scorecard of measures to keep track of the group's aspirations and to reassure those in H1. Also a modified set of initiatives to realise those goals, redesigned to suit the difficult territory ahead. Then the group can be confident that its initial actions will be building the essential infrastructure on which to stand in order to see further into the future: new footing for next steps.

Implemento creates pragmatic hope that there is a possible path by revealing measures which have come from the group itself, not from outside, as a spontaneous response to the H1 to H3 transition tensions. It reveals the essential, right works to be done, the smart moves, the wise initiatives.

This tool in particular has been instrumental in helping schools to turn risk into 'managed risk' and therefore to attempt innovation that previously looked far too scary. In other words, to be the adventurers they always wanted to be. When the first step in the conversation is to ask 'what is the worst that could happen?' and the process then treats the answers seriously, everyone is reassured.

Results

A year after first introducing these approaches into schools, local authorities and community learning settings, the Inspectorate evaluated the results. They devised a special version of the normal school inspection process to generate 'Impact Reports' for the first participating schools. They asked each participating school to complete a self-evaluation on the use of this new approach and the results it has stimulated. They then visited the school with a team of three people – a schools Inspector, an 'associate assessor' (usually another headteacher) and somebody from the local government education department who knew the school in question - for a day of activities and interviews to validate the findings.

The evaluation reports (about fifteen in all at the time of writing, including examples of using The Three Horizons Kit and the change management approaches outlined above in community learning settings outside school) suggest to the Inspectorate three broad outcomes in participating schools:

- a shift in mindset resulting in a belief that it is possible to implement radical change

Practical Approaches To Transformation

- a new capacity for leadership at all levels now that people can get a sense of where they want to go and how to get there
- an impact on confidence and skills for learning and for life amongst pupils themselves using these approaches.

Those are the impacts observed and reported. As for the method, according to the testimony of headteachers involved so far, what is supporting them is a combination of three elements, none of which would be effective on its own:

- the three horizons framework opens up a conversation about the future and develops a refreshed sense of direction;
- the simple and intuitive change tools enable action;
- the school inspector now provides a 'critical friend' able to make useful connections with relevant knowledge, other schools, etc. and a source of non-judgemental advice and encouragement.

Most impressive of all, the students themselves are now taking to these tools with gusto. Three horizons is being used in the classroom as a framework for understanding the dynamics of change in all kinds of areas. Pupils are being invited in to three horizons and Implemento sessions with staff and report above all how the frameworks make them equal participants in the conversation. Pupils from one of the first schools to adopt the approach are now touring other schools in the area to pass on their new-found process skills to their peers. They also used the tools to manage a strategic conversation amongst all the teachers from the region at their annual conference. Transformative innovation is under way.

The Policy Framework

Making Space for Pragmatic Visionaries

Clearly, suitably supported, there is a lot that individual schools and education authorities can do. Our work – particularly with energetic and visionary school leaders – has shown this. But in a state-dominated universal education system, local action will always come up eventually against the H1 constraints of the national policy framework. That needs to be adapted for transition too.

So how might national policy in any country flex and adapt over time so that it is more supportive of the pragmatic visionaries already hard at work on transformative innovation in the existing system? They, after all, are the leaders of change – and they are more numerous and more widespread in the system than many would credit. As one participant in our workshops expressed it, there is significant 'latent innovation' in the system, waiting to emerge and shine brightly once the conditions are right.

Our work suggests an effective policy framework for educational reform needs to facilitate the following six features:

1. **A compelling vision of the third horizon.**
   Without this, all 'innovation' will be sucked back towards making the existing system work 'better' (usually more efficiently). That has been the fate of many educational reform movements to date – churning the surface whilst leaving deep structures unchanged. It is a fundamental government responsibility to keep the strategic conversation about the H3 vision alive and dynamic as the environment continues to change. *Curriculum for Excellence* in Scotland is a good start. But the task of visioning and taking the long view is not over with the publication of the policy framework. Maintaining active discussion about H3 is an integral part of effective implementation.

2. **Encouragement for the early adopters.**
It is not only the absence of a compelling vision that has hindered previous educational reforms. Fundamentally it is the power of the status quo, business-as-usual systems, institutions and assumptions, to hold back, rein in, capture and co-opt innovation that might otherwise have pointed to a different future. This tendency is often exacerbated by overly mechanical school governance arrangements, emphasising the managerial over other mindsets. As Ted Kolderie puts it, referring to the US system, 'the regulated public utility arrangement has made public education an inert institution'. Good schools work more like villages than factories. They are multi-layered, often apparently chaotic, unpredictable, not amenable to micro-management, ordered and ultimately channelled via an agreement – often implicit – on ethos, values and purpose. This can provide a highly creative environment. Hence the policy framework needs to know how to pay special attention to early adopters,[19] advanced practitioners, pioneers. The worry for managerial policy-makers is that encouraging the visionaries will fragment and diversify what is intended to be a universal system. Hence 'if we cannot do it for everyone, we should not do it for anyone'. That is an entrenched mindset utterly at odds with the dynamism demanded by the modern world. To overcome it, it is helpful to treat universalism and diversity as a dilemma rather than a choice, and design a policy framework to encourage generative resolution rather than compromise.

3. **A realistic view of the policy landscape.**
We believe previous programmes of education reform have failed to realise their visionary intentions at least in part because they have not reckoned with the power of the sunk infrastructure to constrain innovation.

The real challenge is not simply to innovate, but to do so in such a way that longer-term evolution of the system results – i.e. introducing the new in ways that allow it to flourish *in the presence of the old*. Policy must acknowledge the real tensions and dilemmas of change, where both the existing system and the imagined future have merit and value. And it must deliberately free up some of the intellectual, physical and financial resources currently locked in to the maintenance and improvement of the existing system to support second horizon innovation with third horizon aspirations – seeding creative resolution of the dilemmas even while the bulk of funding goes towards 'keeping the lights on'.

4. **Strategic exemplification.**
Policy for innovation often follows a simple model of providing dedicated funds to support pilot projects, coupled with investment in 'sharing best practice'. The weakness in such a model can be a lack of strategic direction. With a third horizon vision and a realistic view of the policy landscape, it is possible to be much more intentional about the kind of innovations that are supported, identified and shared. We need examples of third horizon practice in the present – to inspire us. And examples of second horizon innovation that have the potential to ease the transition from the first horizon toward the third. We call this 'strategic exemplification' – the highlighting of examples that are not just novel, different or interesting, but have true *strategic significance* in the context of a stated third horizon vision. The opportunities offered by web 2.0 are revolutionising the knowledge-sharing part of such a strategy – increasingly through Scotland's national intranet for education 'GLOW' and countless other facilities like the TeachMeet wiki or East Lothian's Edubuzz or the numerous groups that gather on Twitter. Equally we must recognise

the inherent limitations of 'sharing best practice' – typically associated with incremental improvement. Transformative innovation is about inspiring not replicating – which suggests much greater use of experiential learning journeys as a way of encouraging growth and development. These journeys need not be far from home.

5. **Systems of support.**
   We know how to support a policy framework for standards-based reform. Follow the four box model shown above (page 23) and it will lead to improvement – if only within the confines of the existing system. The case we argue in this book is that such an approach is necessary but not sufficient. We must also support more visionary, system-shifting practice. That means providing the people who are entrusted with making the shift happen – school leaders, local authorities, others – with the necessary tools and supports to interpret the vision and the challenge in their own contexts. That is different from providing top-down 'guidance'. The Kit that IFF has developed to enable school leaders, local authorities, pupils, parents, governing bodies, policy makers and anyone else engaged in educational reform to have a structured strategic conversation around the three horizons framework is an example of the kind of support that is necessary. So too is the suite of change management approaches that is going down so well in Scotland's schools. There is little point distributing the authority to innovate without the tools and processes that will allow busy professionals to use it in the course of their other duties.

6. **Evaluation.**
   This is one dilemma that must be addressed head on. Transformative innovation cannot be evaluated simply according to the standards and processes of

H1. But it must be evaluated – not only to encourage the innovators, but to retain credibility within the structures of H1. That is not easy – as we have discussed. But it is a challenge that must be addressed. As Jim Collins says in his *Good to Great for the Social Sector*, anyone who says that their version of success cannot be measured is guilty of intellectual laziness. Thus an essential element of the practical transition towards an H3 vision should be a disciplined approach to self-evaluation which recognises the value of experience and narrative alongside more conventional data. The measures derived naturally from the conversations involved in the Implemento process (page 48) are a good example of how to incorporate evaluation into the innovation programme. At the same time any system needs to recognise the reality of the dilemma dance, rather than assuming a simple linear model of incremental progress towards the third horizon. Transformational change does not happen in that step-by-step fashion. The evaluation framework itself will need to be an innovation and a strategic example to others.

All of these points are inter-related. Without a vision of the future and an appreciation of the power of present structures we cannot even start to conceive of the kinds of transformative innovation necessary to shift education systems. And that innovation will be short-lived unless it is acknowledged and supported in terms other than those in the familiar playbook of standards-based reform.

And finally

TRANSFORMATIVE change in education is an ambitious goal. But it is a necessary one. It will take years, decades even, to achieve.

We hope that the ideas and insights described in this book, the analysis of how and why transformation is held

The Policy Framework

back in most systems, and the three horizons Kit and the supportive approaches we have developed through our work in Scotland may provide some encouragement for those on the journey.

The initial goal can be modest. As Alexander Pope said in his *Essay on Man* 'not to go back is somewhat to advance'. That is especially true in the field of education where the forces of conservatism and incremental improvement are very difficult to resist. By seeding and supporting pockets of future practice and resisting the siren calls of the first horizon we might at last start to shift our education systems not into the future but into a fuller accommodation with the ever-flowing present.

Endnotes

1. McKinsey and Company, 'How the world's most improved school systems keep getting better', Mona Mourshed, Chinezi Chijioke and Michael Barber, November 2010
2. See http://www.ltscotland.org.uk/curriculumforexcellence/
3. The issue of '21st century competencies' is taken up in Maureen O'Hara and Graham Leicester, *Dancing at the Edge: competence, culture and organisation in the 21st century,* Triarchy Press, 2012
4. The more familiar term is 'best practice' – which suggests a coming together around proven method while 'next practice' suggests a bold step into something novel and untested.
5. See *The Fischbowl* for more details: http://thefischbowl.blogspot.com/2007/06/did-you-know-20.html
6. *European Journal of Education*, Volume 42, Issue 2, June 2007
7. McKinsey and Company, *op.cit.*
8. Larry Cuban, *How Teachers Taught: Constancy and Change in American Classrooms, 1890-1990,* Teachers College Press, 1993
9. Barack Obama, *The Audacity of Hope: Thoughts on Reclaiming the American Dream*, Canongate Books, 2007
10. See http://www.internationalfuturesforum.com/projects.php?id=26
11. Mehrdad Baghai, Stephen Coley, and David White, *The Alchemy of Growth*, Perseus, 1999
12. See http://www.internationalfuturesforum.com/three-horizons and Andrew Curry and Anthony Hodgson, 'Seeing in Multiple Horizons: Connecting Futures to Strategy', *Journal of Futures Studies*, August 2008, 13(1): 1 - 20

13 Note that the values base of the education system is seldom questioned. But in practice it is possible to detect an ongoing struggle between a set of values based on serving the needs of the economy and a broader set of values relating to human growth and wellbeing.

14 See 'What have the unborn ever done for me: complexity, uncertainty and tragic choices in the governance of the future' in James McCormick (Ed) *Innovation in Public Services*, Scottish Council Foundation, 2003

15 'Standards-based systemic reform' is a US movement, initiated by an influential essay by Mike Smith and Jennifer O'Day ('Systemic School Reform' in Susan Fuhrman and Betty Malen (eds.) *The Politics of Curriculum and Testing*, Falmer Press, 1991). It has since been challenged as essentially conservative and lacking in innovation, for example by the charter school movement. For more information see http://www.educationevolving.org/ and in particular Ted Kolderie's critique of so-called 'systemic reform'.

16 See http://www.deseco.admin.ch/

17 See Maureen O'Hara and Graham Leicester, *op. cit.*

18 June Delano, 'The Power of the Status Quo: a story about executive development' at http://www.internationalfuturesforum.com/fol/june_delano.pdf

19 The term is taken from Geoffrey Moore's influential book *Crossing the Chasm: Marketing and Selling High-tech Products to Mainstream Customers*, (1991, revised 1999). The book identifies different market segments in taking up new disruptive technologies: innovators, early adopters, early majority, late majority and laggards. The 'chasm' lies between early adopters (visionaries) who want to try something new and the early majority (pragmatists) who want to adopt something that works better than what they have already.

IFF Members

Martin Albrow	*Formerly Professor of Sociology, State University of New York, Stony Brook, author 'The Global Age: state and society beyond modernity'*
Ruth Anderson	*Chief Executive, Barataria Foundation, Scotland*
Tony Beesley	*Conceptual artist and cartoonist*
Max Boisot (died 2011)	*Professor at ESADE, University of Ramon Llull in Barcelona and Associate Fellow at the Said Business School, University of Oxford. Author of 'Knowledge Assets: securing competitive advantage in the information economy'*
Roberto Carneiro	*Former Education Minister, President of Grupo Forum, Portugal, UNESCO International Commission on Education for the Twenty-first Century*
Napier Collyns	*Co-founder, Global Business Network (GBN), San Francisco, USA*
Thomas Corver	*Corver Management Consultancy, former strategy coordinator at ING bank, The Netherlands*
Pamela Deans	*IFF recorder and ForthRoad Limited, Scotland*
Roanne Dods	*Artistic Director PAL, former Director, Jerwood Charitable Foundation*
Kate Ettinger	*Senior Fellow, Center for Health Professions, UCSF; Health Care Ethics Consulant-Mediator & Social Change Educator, San Francisco, USA*

Jim Ewing	*Independent designer of practical strategies and methods for sustained transformational achievement in uncertain times. Author of 'TransforMAP' and 'Council', conceptware and software for organisational development, Seattle USA*
Brian Goodwin (died 2009)	*Schumacher College, Devon and Santa Fe Institute, author 'How the Leopard Changed its Spots. the evolution of complexity'*
Bo Gyllenpalm	*President SITSERV AB, Sweden and faculty member Fielding Graduate University, USA*
Mike Hambly	*Former Chief Executive, Digital Animations Group, Glasgow*
Margaret Hannah	*Deputy Director of Public Health, NHS Fife, Scotland*
Pat Heneghan	*Director, ForthRoad Limited, Scotland*
David Hodgson	*Co-founder, The Idea Hive and Connective, San Francisco, USA*
Rebecca Hodgson	*Researcher, International Futures Forum*
Tony Hodgson	*Director, Decision Integrity Ltd, World Modelling Research International Futures Forum*
Robert Horn	*Visiting Scholar in the Human Sciences and Technology Advanced Research Institute (H-STAR) at Stanford University and CEO of MacroVU Inc.*
Kees van der Heijden	*Professor at Templeton College, Oxford, author 'Scenarios: the art of strategic conversation'*
Adam Kahane	*Reos Partners and University of Oxford, author of 'Solving Tough Problems', 'Power and Love' and 'Transformative Scenario Planning'*
Pat Kane	*Writer, theorist and musician, Glasgow, author 'The Play Ethic'*

Eamonn Kelly	*President, Global Business Network. Author 'Powerful Times: rising to the challenge of our uncertain world'*
Rajiv Kumar	*Director General, Federation of Indian Chambers of Commerce and Industry (FICCI) New Delhi*
Graham Leicester	*Director, International Futures Forum*
David Lorimer	*Programme Director, Scientific and Medical Network, Scotland,*
Charles Lowe	*Consultant, Former head of e-government, BT*
Wendy Luhabe	*Bridging the Gap, South Africa, author 'Defining Moments: experiences of black executives in South Africa's workplace'*
Andrew Lyon	*Converger, International Futures Forum*
James McCormick	*Scotland Adviser, Joseph Rowntree Foundation*
Arun Maira	*Member, Planning Commission, Government of India*
Wolfgang Michalski	*WM International, formerly Director, OECD International Futures Programme, author 'Capitalising on Change in a Globalising World'*
Maureen O'Hara	*Chair of Psychology Department, National University La Jolla, CA and President Emerita, Saybrook Graduate School, San Francisco*
Aftab Omer	*President, Meridian University, California*
Ian Page	*Former Research Manager / Futurist, HP Corporate Labs.*
David Peat	*Theoretical physicist and Director of the Pari Center for the New Learning, Tuscany, Italy*
Maria Pereira	*Clinton Climate Initiative and former investment manager*

Noah Raford	*Department of Urban Studies and Planning MIT and Special Adviser, Office of the Prime Minister, UAE*
Nick Rengger	*Professor of Political Theory and International Relations, University of St Andrews, author 'International Relations, Political Theory and the Problem of Order'*
Vineeta Shanker	*Independent Researcher on faiths in the global economy, previously project director World Faiths Development Dialogue*
Bill Sharpe	*Independent researcher in science, technology and society; Visiting Professor, University of the West of England, author 'Economies of Life'*
Daniel Wahl	*Transition Catalyst & Resilience Research, International Futures Forum (Spain, Germany, UK), former Director of Findhorn College*
Jennifer Williams	*Artist and former Director, Centre for Creative Communities, UK*
Mark Woodhouse	*Professor of Philosophy Emeritus at Georgia State University, USA, author 'Paradigm Wars: worldviews for a new age'*
Chris Yapp	*Specialist in technology, policy and innovation and Senior Associate Fellow at the Institute of Governance and Public Management, Warwick Business School.*

Publishers

TRIARCHY Press publishes in the field of organisational and social praxis: the process by which a theory or skill is applied, practised or embodied. We look for the best new thinking on the organisations and social structures we work and live in.

The name 'Triarchy' comes from Gerard Fairtlough's Triarchy Theory, which challenges the hegemony of hierarchy in organisations and puts forward two alternative ways of organising power and responsibility in order to get things done: heterarchy and responsible autonomy.

We publish books, pamphlets, articles, a game and an Idioticon (a glossary) about innovative approaches to designing and steering organisations, the public sector, teams, society ... and the creative lives of individuals. Our publications offer a number of different but related approaches to organisational issues from the fields of systems thinking, design thinking, innovation, cultural theory, complexity, somatics and leadership studies.

Triarchy Press works in partnership with IFF to publish pamphlets and books that share IFF's learning with the global community. To date these are:
In Search of the Missing Elephant by Don Michael
Economies of Life by Bill Sharpe
Ten Things to Do in a Conceptual Emergency by Graham Leicester and Maureen O'Hara
Beyond Survival by Graham Leicester
Ready for Anything by Anthony Hodgson
Dancing at the Edge by Maureen O'Hara and Graham Leicester

tp

www.triarchypress.com
info@triarchypress.com

International Futures Forum

INTERNATIONAL Futures Forum (IFF) is a non-profit organisation established to support a transformative response to complex and confounding challenges and to restore the capacity for effective action in today's powerful times.

At the heart of IFF is a deeply informed inter-disciplinary and international network of individuals from a range of backgrounds covering a wide range of diverse perspectives, countries and disciplines. The group meets as a learning community as often as possible, including in plenary session. And it seeks to apply its learning in practice.

IFF takes on complex, messy, seemingly intractable issues – notably in the arenas of health, learning, governance and enterprise – where paradox, ambiguity and complexity characterise the landscape, where rapid change means yesterday's solution no longer works, where long-term needs require a long-term logic and where only genuine innovation has any chance of success.

Authors

GRAHAM Leicester is Director of International Futures Forum. He is a former member of HM Diplomatic Service and has subsequently developed a special interest and wide experience in areas of governance, innovation, education and the arts. He is the author, with Maureen O'Hara, of *Dancing at the Edge: Competence, Culture and Organization in the 21st Century*.

KEIR Bloomer has been a Director of Education and Chief Executive of a local authority. He is now an educational consultant, chair of the Court of Queen Margaret University, Edinburgh and chair of the Tapestry Partnership.

DENIS Stewart is a former research chemist in UK universities and a science teacher in Northern Ireland. He has worked in executive leadership positions in national educational development agencies in Wales and Scotland and latterly as co-Director of an educational consultancy, CELT Associates. Now in his 'post-professional' phase of life, he divides much of his time between personal study, travel and various voluntary commitments.

JIM Ewing has worked in industry for over thirty years articulating design, learning, and transformation as one whole rather than three separate endeavours. His current suite of practices arose from guiding individuals and their tribes through intense, inner and outer driven change, as they reinvented themselves and their work. Jim's early career as a systems engineer and rocket scientist left the marks of efficiency. His practices assist the upside by materially reducing the downside of wasted angst, time and resources as people confront, resist and get to grips with the change of their minds, their choices and their stories. Jim has consulted in scores of large corporations and taught his methods widely. His Tallpine Community of learners, practitioners and professionals is a portal to his artful guidance for transformative living, innovation and leadership.

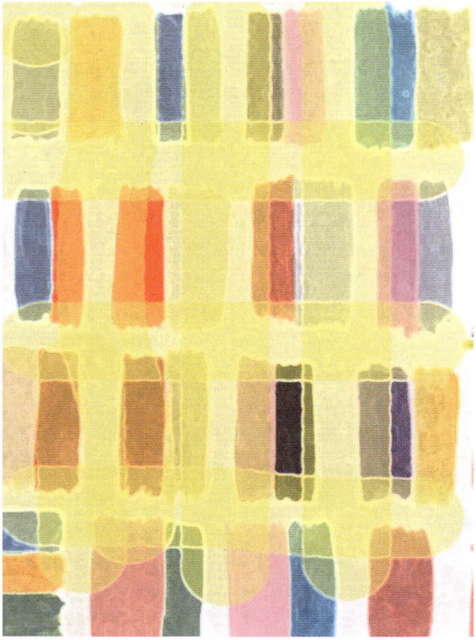